cATMaS cARoLS

CATMAS CAROLS

BY LAURIE LOUGHLIN
ILLUSTRATED BY MARY ROSS

CHRONICLE BOOKS
SAN FRANCISCO

Printed in Hong Kong.

Book and cover design by Carrie Leeb.

Library of Congress Cataloging-in-Publication Data
Catmas Carols / by Laurie Loughlin ; illustrated by Mary Ross.
p.   cm.
ISBN: 0-8118-0237-X
1. Cats—Humor. 2. Carols, English—Humor 3. Christmas—
Humor. 4. Parodies. I. Ross, Mary, 1947- . II. Title.
PN6231.C23L68 1993
818' .5402—dc20   92-34649
                                                CIP

Distributed in Canada by Raincoast Books,
8680 Cambie Street, Vancouver, B.C. V6P 6M9

10 9 8 7

Chronicle Books
85 Second Street
San Francisco, CA 94105

In memory of Max, beloved friend.

I would like to thank:

-my parents, Richard and Laura Loughlin,
for placing my childhood rocking chair next
to the record player and encouraging my
love of songs;

-my editor, Charlotte Stone, for caring so
much about this book;

-Mary Ross for her impish illustrations;

-my friends, John Rumble, Christa Shreffler
and Bob Reddig for coming up with some of
the parody titles;

-and all cats (especially Greta and Penelope)
for being the splendid individuals they are.

coNtents

WE THREE CATS

of
ORIENT
ARE

We three cats of Orient are
Terrified to get in the car.
Why go out for celebrating?
We'll stay right where we are. Oooh—

CHORUS:
Home is heaven. Home is good.
Home is where we get our food.
Why go out for Christmas parties?
Frankly we're not in the mood.

We're not happy with a trip yet.
Seems they always end at the vet.
These excursions are diversions
We'd just as soon forget. Oooh—

(Repeat CHORUS)

We three cats are Siamese,
Himalayan, and Tonkinese.
Bring us gifts of meat with gravy
And mild kinds of cheese. Oooh—

(Repeat CHORUS)

("We Three Kings of Orient Are")

OH, CHRISTMAS TREE

Oh, C

Oh, Christmas

ornaments shi

I want to wha

my paw And

when they hit

Oh, Christmas

Oh, Christmas

ornaments shi

hristmas Tree!

Tree! 🔴 Your

ne temptingly.

ck them with

grab them

the floor.

Tree! ("O Tannenbaum")

Tree! 🔴 Your

ne temptingly.

AWAKE iN a CAt BEd

Awake in a cat bed,
She can't go to sleep.
She's thinking of cat toys
That she'd like to keep.
She's seen them in catalogs
And on TV,
And she's left her Christmas list
Pinned to the tree.

A catnip-filled heart and
A long piece of string,
A large kitty condo
With everything,
Cat videotapes and
A brush for her fur,
She's hoping that Santa
Will bring these for her.

("Away in a Manger")

THE FiRSt MEoW

The first meow,
The angels did say,
Was to certain white Persians
On rugs where they lay,
On rugs where they
Lay trying to sleep,
Having dreams about cat life
That were so deep.
Meow, meow, meow, meow.
They'll get to do what they want, somehow.
Meow, meow, meow, meow.
They'll get to do what they want, somehow.

("The First Noel")

WReCk thE hAlls

Wreck the halls with two cats running,
Fa-la-la-la-la . . . la-la-la-la.
Fur goes flying, lamps get done in,
Fa-la-la-la-la . . . la-la-la-la.
Tumbling swiftly down the stairway,
Fa-la-la, la-la-la, la, la, la.
Woe to those who get in their way,
Fa-la-la-la-la . . . la-la-la-la.

("Deck the Halls")

i sAw tHreE cAts

I saw three cats prance merrily
On Christmas Day, on Christmas Day,
I saw three cats prance merrily
On Christmas Day, in the morning.

They played a game of hide-and-seek
On Christmas Day, on Christmas Day,
They played a game of hide-and-seek
Oh Christmas Day, in the morning.

And rolled around on the floor with glee
On Christmas Day, on Christmas Day,
And rolled around on the floor with glee
On Christmas Day, in the morning.

Greta, Max, and Penelope
On Christmas Day, on Christmas Day,
Greta, Max, and Penelope
On Christmas Day, in the morning.

To watch them brings such joy to me
On Christmas Day, on Christmas Day,
To watch them brings such joy to me
On Christmas Day, in the morning.

("I Saw Three Ships")

oH, CoME

aLL

yE

FuRfuL

Oh, come all ye furful,
Hungry and well-rested,
Oh, come ye, oh, come ye to
The master bedroom.
Come and behold them
Snoring loudly 'neath the sheets,
For now it's time to wake them,
For now it's time to wake them,
For now it's time to wake them
On this Christmas morn.

Meow, choirs of felines,
Meow in expectation.
Meow till you get your Mom
And Dad out of bed.
Glory to food
In the cat dish.
Oh, come let us enjoy it.
Oh, come let us enjoy it.
Oh, come let us enjoy it,
Breakfast at last!

("Oh, Come All Ye Faithful")

20

Oh, coMe all y

HuNgry ANd

oH,

ye

ThE

er

coN

d B

SnoRiNg Lou

for Now it's t

We want some tu

We want some tu

We want some tu

We want some tu

Beef would be ni

(Repeat several times, incre

the tempo each time.)

na and chicken.

na and chicken.

na and chicken.

na, chicken,

ce, too.

sing

GooD CAts

iN thE hOUSe

Good cats in the house are bad
When their Mom's not looking,
Stick their noses everywhere
Just to see what's cooking.
When their claws need polishing,
Shred the couch and love seat.
They don't heed admonishing,
But their misdeeds repeat!

Good cats in the house are sad
When they feel neglected.
They will yowl without respite
Or act cool and affected.
Special love at Christmastime
Is what they require,
That we pet them ceaselessly,
Their good looks to admire!

("Good King Wenceslas")

Hₐₗₗₑₗᵤⱼₐₕ Pₒᵤᵣ Uₛ

Hallelujah! Hallelujah!
The food bag is tilted. Hallelujah!
Hallelujah! Hallelujah!
Food cascading, coming towards us. Hallelujah!

Is it Purina Chow? Perhaps Meow Mix?
Hallelujah! Hallelujah! Hallelujah! Hallelujah!
Alpo or Friskies? All have their taste kicks.
Hallelujah! Hallelujah! Hallelujah! Hallelujah!

And we shall eat forever and ever.
And we shall eat forever and ever.

Hail, Nine Lives,
Hallelujah! Hallelujah! Hallelujah! Hallelujah!
And Happy Cat.
Hallelujah! Hallelujah! Hallelujah! Hallelujah!
Whiskas jives
Hallelujah! Hallelujah! Hallelujah! Hallelujah!
With my habitat.
Hallelujah! Hallelujah! Hallelujah! Hallelujah!

Hallelujah!

("Hallelujah Chorus")

iT cAMe UpoN a MIdNIGhT CAt

It came upon a midnight cat
Whose fur was black and bold,
As he sat under the carport in
December though it was cold,
That he was lord of his backyard.
The neighborhood cats agree,
For, when he hisses, they turn and leave
His yard immediately.

("It Came Upon a Midnight Clear")

COLLAR BELLS

CHORUS:
Collar bells, collar bells,
Ringing 'round the block,
Christmas Eve is party time,
And we cats like to rock.
Collar bells, collar bells,
Ringing 'round the block,
Christmas Eve is party time,
We're counting down the clock.

We wait out on the porch
And sing amewsing songs.
We know that Santa Claws
Will be here before long.
The chimney has been swept
To ease his passage down.
We'll entertain the reindeer
While he puts the presents 'round. Oh,

(Repeat CHORUS)

Our families are asleep,
But not we watchful cats.
While waiting we engage
In elementary spats,
Deciding who'll be boss
And shake ol' Santa's hand.
This holiday excitement's
Almost more than we can stand. Oh,

(Repeat CHORUS)

("Jingle Bells")

gO, sMeLL iT AT thE foUNtaINs

When I was a kitten,
 my Mama mewed to me,
"You'll have to find your food yourself
 when there's no other way.
Go, smell it at the fountains,
Out on the docks, in market stalls.
Go, smell it at the fountains.
Our Christmas fish is spawned."

Now I am in charge of
 the Christmas feast for cats.
They know that I'm an expert sniff
 at finding this and that.
"Go, smell it at the fountains,
Out on the docks, in market stalls.
Go, smell it at the fountains.
Our Christmas fish is spawned."

("Go, Tell It on The Mountains")

BARK! THE NEIGHBORS'

DOGS

WILL

SOUND

Bark! The neighbors' dogs will sound
When they see us spin around.
They can really make it hard
For cats to play in the yard.

Canine cousins are a puzzle.
Santa, please bring each a muzzle.
We can't wait for the time when
Silent nights are here again.

Bark! The neighbors' dogs will sound.
May Christmas peace and love abound!

("Hark! The Herald Angels Sing")

Insis

With rubs and

It's time to cudd

those you love th

on laps and sid

Stretch your pa

toward the sky.

bliss. You were

ent cats, rejoice

urrs and voice.

le close ❧ With

e most. ❧ Jump

ways lie.

ws out

me-YOW

PURR-R-R-R

("Good Christian Men, Rejoice")

Petting is such

born for this.

O! Little Town of Cat Mayhem

O! Little town of Cat Mayhem,
What mischiefs among you lie?
They look angelic in their sleep,
But there's nothing they won't try.
And in the dark night shineth
Alert, translucent eyes
As they attack the Christmas stockings
Carrying off the prize.

("O! Little Town of Bethlehem")

cArol
of
the
sMelLs

Hark! How the smells,
Sweet Christmas smells,
All seem to say
"It's a buffet."
Hot food and cold
For young and old,
Never have we
Sniffed with such glee,
Platters and bowls,
Meatballs and molds.
Big jumbo shrimp
Make me an imp.
Cheese canapes
And bouillabaisse,
Eggnog to drink,
We're on the brink!
Tabletop heights
Filled with delights,
Though they're so high,
We have to try.

("Carol of the Bells")

Jump on the counter!
Jump on the table!
We'll pounce wherever
Our paws are able.

Merry, merry, merry, merry Christmas!
Merry, merry, merry, merry Christmas!

Scents that are there
Waft through the air,
Leading us to
Morsels to chew. Meow.

Meow, meow, meow, meow,
. . . (hiccup!) . . . . meow.

oh, HOLD Me RiGHt

Oh, hold me right.
Your grasp has got me keeling.
It's whine and squirm time
When you pick me up.
Long have I tried
To let you know my feeling,
That when you lift me,
My life you disrupt!

I'd rather trot
And go about my business.
The grip you've got's
Not popular with me.

Put me down, please.
I need to see the turkey.
Oh, sight divine,
Even though I'm now airborne.
Oh, sight divine!
Let me go! This bird is mine!

("O Holy Night")

GOD REST YE
MERRY, KITTY CATS

God rest ye merry, kitty cats,
Let nothing you dismay.
Remember, lots of yummy food
Is served on Christmas Day,
To save us all from hungry tummies,
Hip, hip, hip hooray!
Oooh, tidings of catnip and joy,
Catnip and joy.
Oooh, tidings of catnip and joy.

("God Rest Ye Merry, Gentlemen")

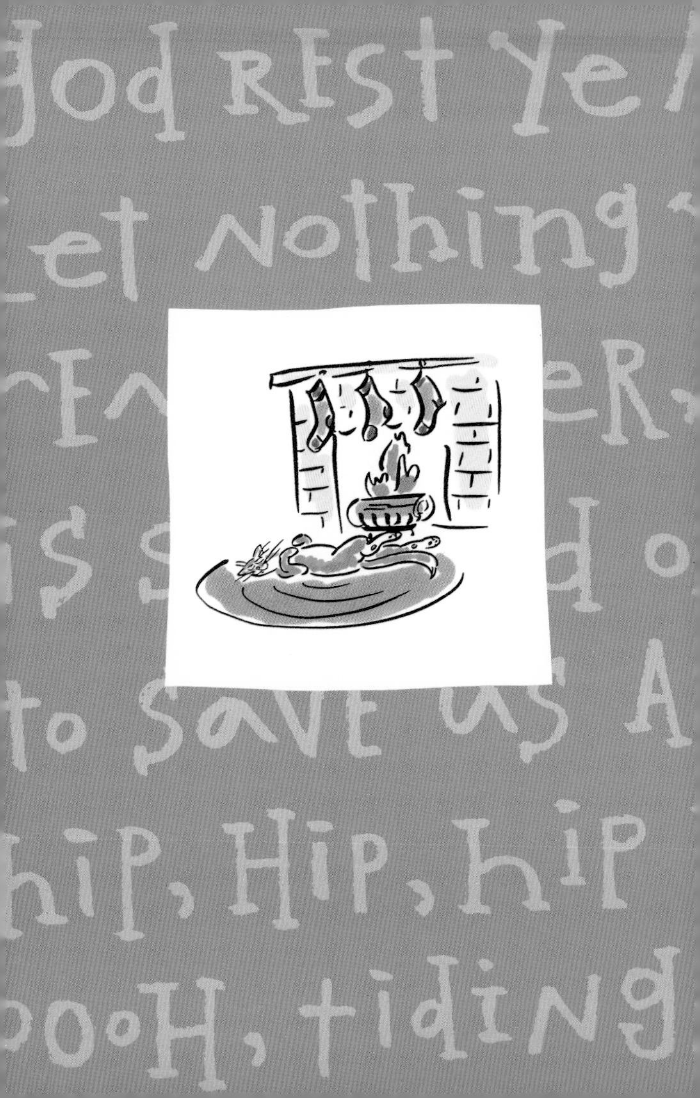
God Rest Ye
Let nothing
to Save us A
hip, Hip, hip
ooH, tiding

Joy

'cause cats are h

all hearts with

everyone prepa

food 🥫 And let th

And let them eat

let, and let them

to the world,

ere. 🥫 They fill

ove. 🥫 Let

e them

em eat their fill,

their fill, 🥫 And

eat their fill.